THE VERY BEST OF
FINGERSTYLE GUITAR

PAGE	TITLE	TRACK
4	AIN'T MISBEHAVIN'	1
2	AULD LANG SYNE	2
10	AVE MARIA	3
14	CANON IN D	4
7	THE CHRISTMAS SONG (CHESTNUTS ROASTING ON AN OPEN FIRE)	5
16	EINE KLEINE NACHTMUSIK	6
20	(EVERYTHING I DO) I DO IT FOR YOU	7
24	THE FIRST NOËL	8
26	THE GIRL FROM IPANEMA (GARÔTA DE IPANEMA)	9
17	IN MY LIFE	10
30	JESU, JOY OF MAN'S DESIRING	11
32	LIBERTY BELL MARCH	12
34	LONGER	13
40	MEMORY	14
37	MISTY	15
44	MY FUNNY VALENTINE	16
47	MY HEART WILL GO ON (LOVE THEME FROM 'TITANIC')	17
54	ODE TO JOY	18
58	POMP AND CIRCUMSTANCE	19
55	ROMANCE	20
60	SATIN DOLL	21
63	SILVER BELLS	22
70	TEARS IN HEAVEN	23
66	UNCHAINED MELODY	24
68	YESTERDAY	25

To access audio visit:
www.halleonard.com/mylibrary

Enter Code
3489-4382-1626-7485

ISBN 978-0-634-05239-2

HAL•LEONARD®
CORPORATION
7777 W. BLUEMOUND RD. P.O. BOX 13819 MILWAUKEE, WI 53213

Visit Hal Leonard Online at
www.halleonard.com

Auld Lang Syne

Words by Robert Burns
Traditional Scottish Melody

Drop D tuning:
(low to high) D-A-D-G-B-E

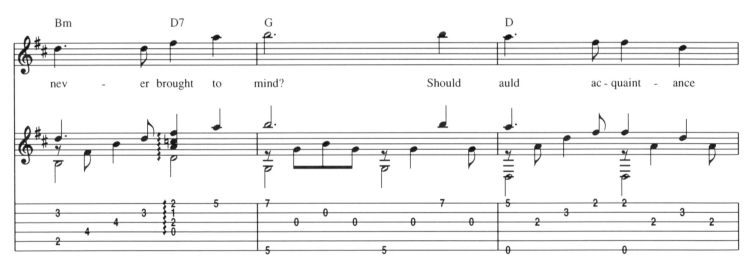

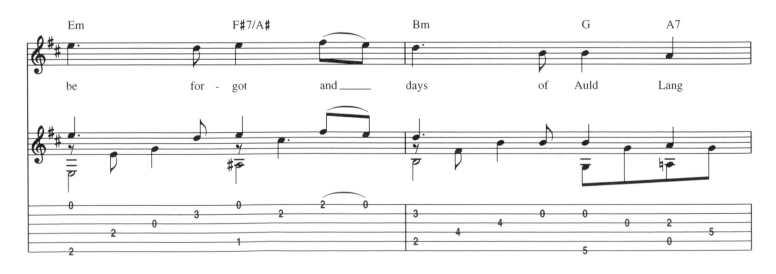

Ain't Misbehavin'

from AIN'T MISBEHAVIN'

Words by Andy Razaf
Music by Thomas "Fats" Waller and Harry Brooks

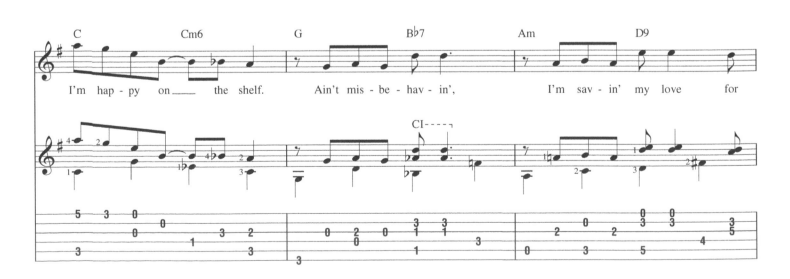

What do I care? Your kiss - es are worth wait - in' for, be -

Outro

lieve me. I don't stay out late, don't care to go. I'm home a - bout eight, just

me and my ra - di - o. Ain't mis - be - hav - in', I'm sav - in' my love for

you. you.

The Christmas Song
(Chestnuts Roasting on an Open Fire)

Music and Lyric by Mel Torme and Robert Wells

Drop D tuning:
(low to high) D-A-D-G-B-E

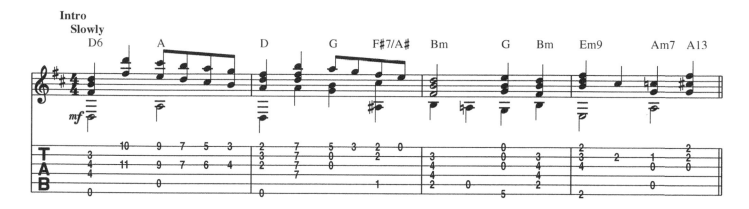

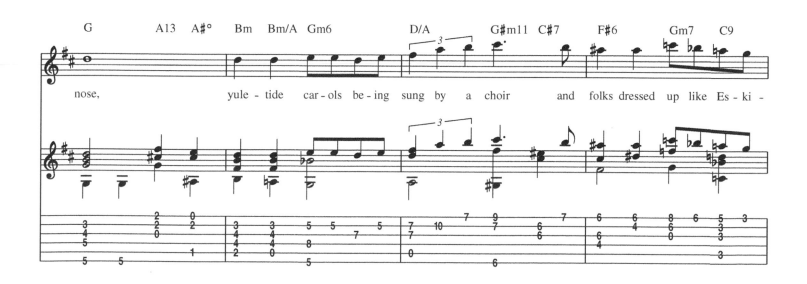

Ave Maria

By Franz Schubert

Drop D tuning:
(low to high) D-A-D-G-B-E

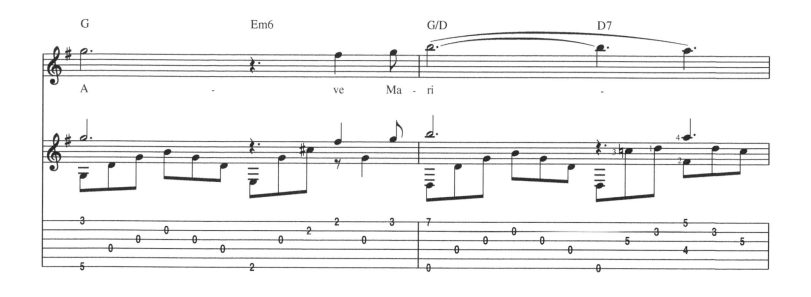

A - ve Ma - ri -

a!

slight rit.

Canon in D

By Johann Pachelbel

Drop D tuning:
(low to high) D-A-D-G-B-E

Moderately

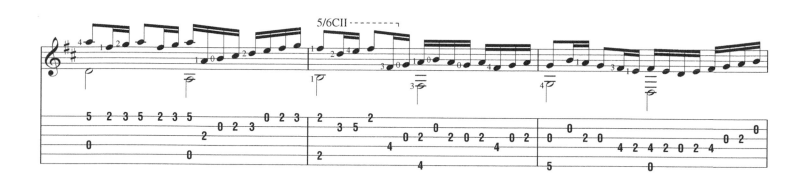

Eine Kleine Nachtmusik

By W.A. Mozart

In My Life

Words and Music by John Lennon and Paul McCartney

(Everything I Do) I Do It for You

from the Motion Picture ROBIN HOOD: PRINCE OF THIEVES

Words and Music by Bryan Adams, Robert John Lange and Michael Kamen

Interlude

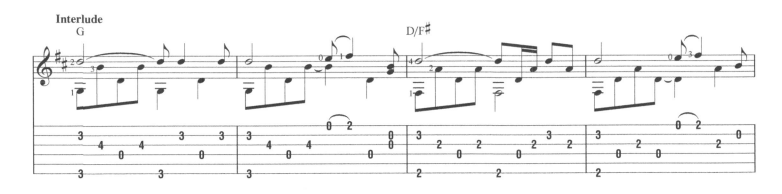

The First Noël

17th Century English Carol
Music from W. Sandys' Christmas Carols

1. The first Noël, the angel did say, was to certain poor
2.-5. *See additional lyrics*

shepherds in fields as they lay. In fields where they lay

keeping their sheep, on a cold winter's night that was so

deep. No - ël, _____ No - ël, No - ël, No - ël,

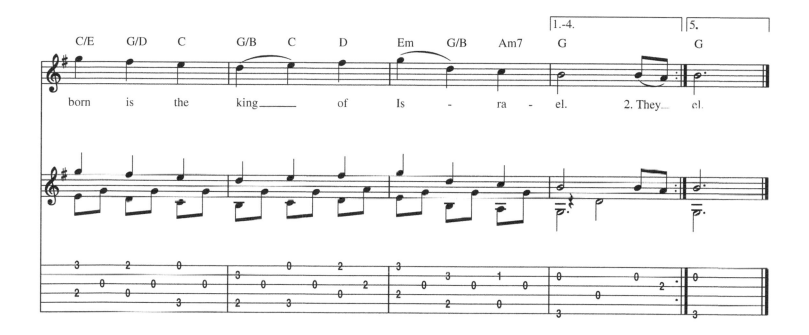

born is the king_____ of Is - ra - el. 2. They_____ el.

Additional Lyrics

2. They looked up and saw a star
   Shining in the East, beyond them far.
   And to the earth it gave great light
   And so it continued both day and night.

3. And by the light of that same star,
   Three wise man came from country far;
   To seek for a king was their intent,
   And to follow the star wherever it went.

4. This star drew nigh to the northwest,
   O'er Bethlehem it took its rest;
   And there it did both stop and stay,
   Right over the place where Jesus lay.

5. Then entered in those wise men three,
   Full reverently upon their knee;
   And offered there in His presence,
   Their gold, and myrrh, and frankincense.

The Girl from Ipanema
(Garôta de Ipanema)

Music by Antonio Carlos Jobim
English Words by Norman Gimbel
Original Words by Vinicius de Moraes

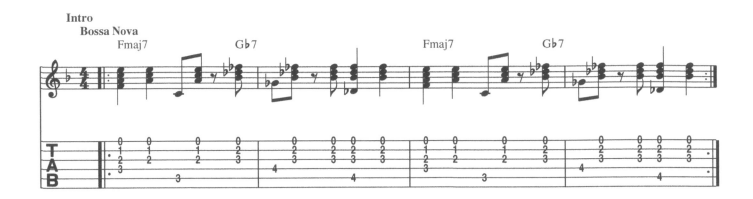

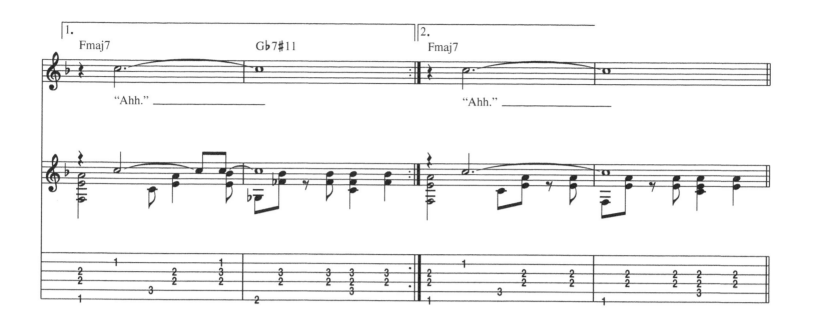

Yes, _____ I would give my heart glad - ly, _____ but each day _

_ as she walks _ to the sea, ____ she looks __ straight a - head __ not at me. _

Verse

3. Tall and tan and young __ and love - ly the girl _

from Ip - a - ne - ma goes walk - ing and when she pas - ses I smile _

but she does-n't see. _____ She just does-n't see,

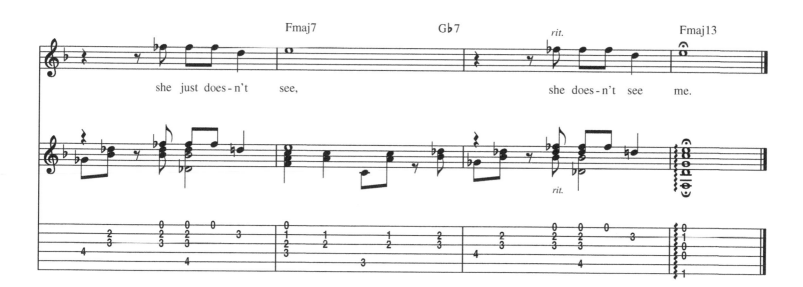

she just does - n't see, she does - n't see me.

Additional Lyrics

2. When she walks it's like a samba
   That swings so smoothe and swags so gentle that
   When she passes, each one she passes goes, "Ahh."

Jesu, Joy of Man's Desiring

By Johann Sebastian Bach

Drop D tuning:
(low to high) D-A-D-G-B-E

Moderately

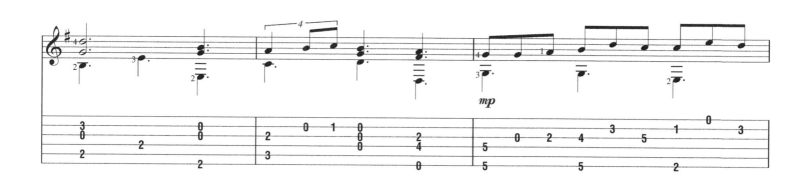

Liberty Bell March

By John Philip Sousa

Drop D tuning:
(low to high) D-A-D-G-B-E

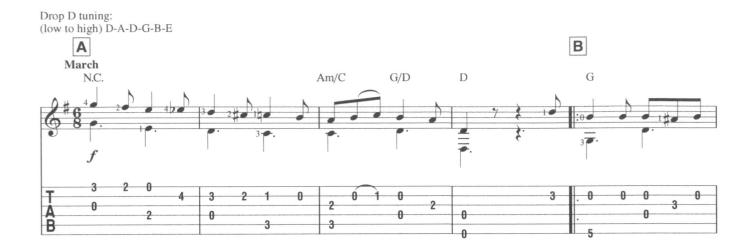

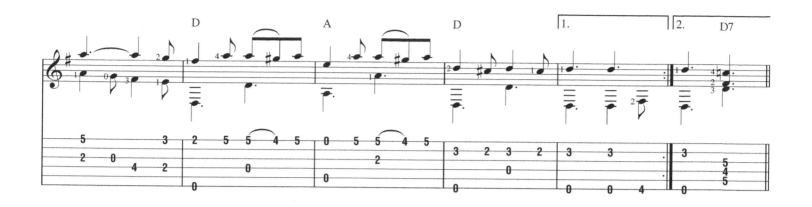

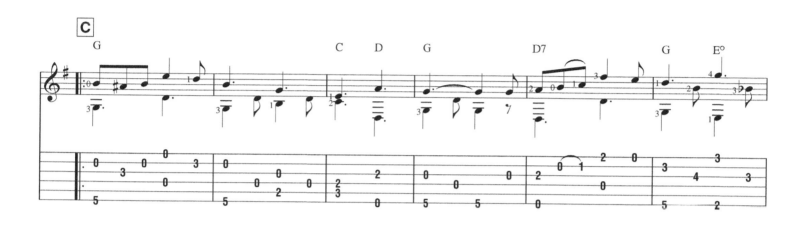

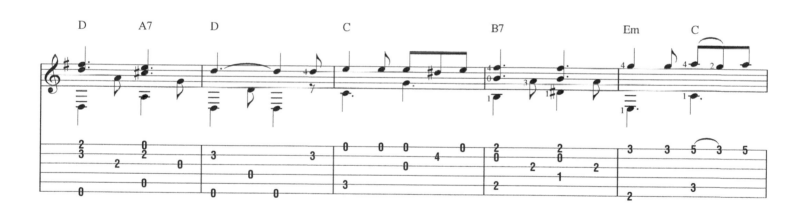

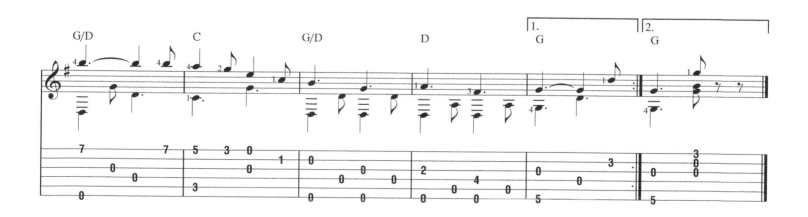

Longer

Words and Music by Dan Fogelberg

Drop D tuning:
(low to high) D-A-D-G-B-E

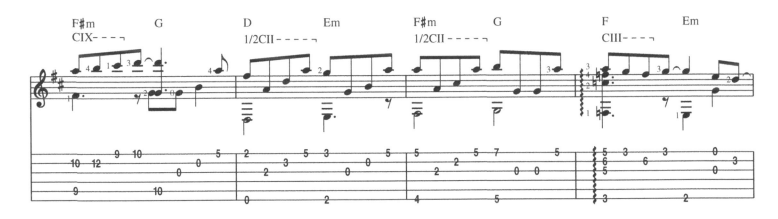

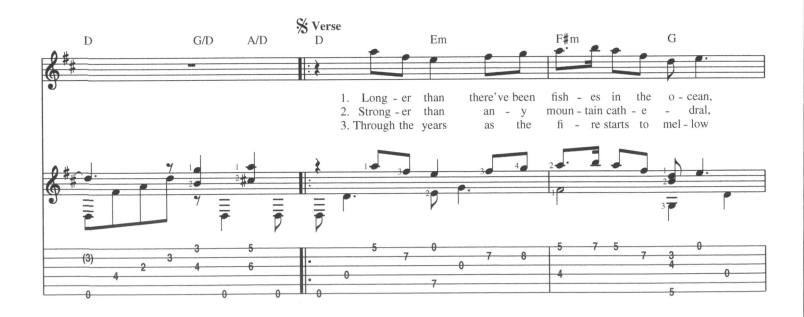

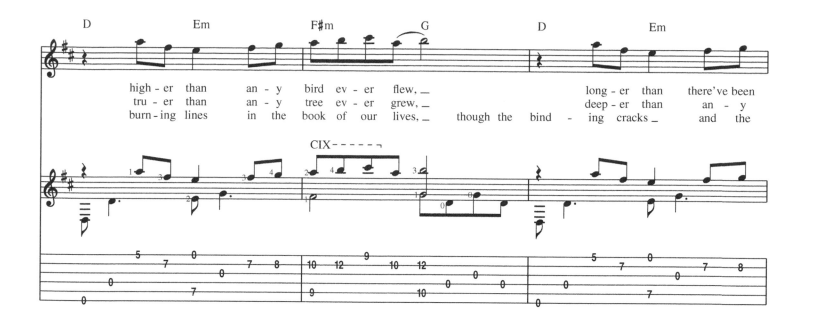

high - er than an - y bird ev - er flew, ___ long - er than there've been
tru - er than an - y tree ev - er grew, ___ deep - er than an - y
burn - ing lines in the book of our lives, ___ though the bind - ing cracks ___ and the

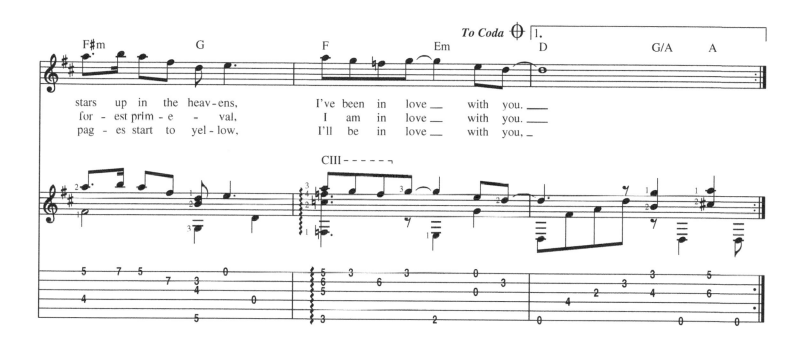

stars up in the heav - ens, I've been in love ___ with you. ___
for - est prim - e - val, I am in love ___ with you. ___
pag - es start to yel - low, I'll be in love ___ with you, ___

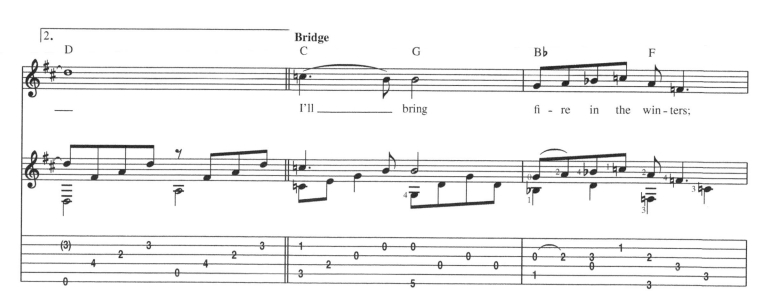

I'll ___ bring fi - re in the win - ters;

D.S. al Coda

Coda

36

Misty

Words by Johnny Burke
Music by Erroll Garner

Memory

from CATS
Music by Andrew Lloyd Webber
Text by Trevor Nunn after T.S. Eliot

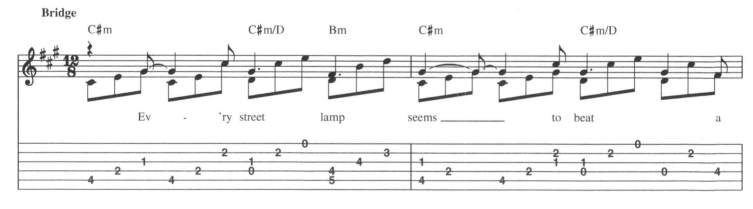

dawn   comes   to-night   will   be   a   mem-o-ry   too, _____   and   a

new   day _____   will _____   be - gin.

Interlude

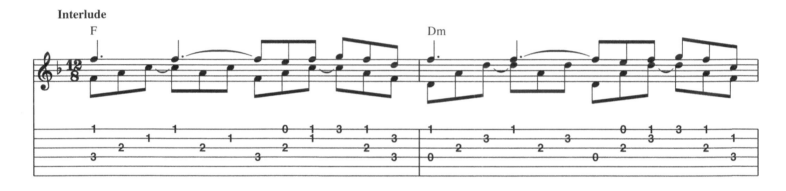

Bridge

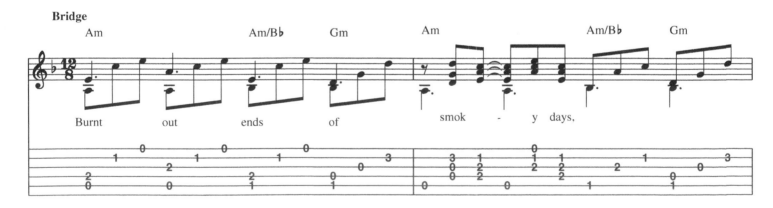

Burnt   out   ends   of   smok - y days,

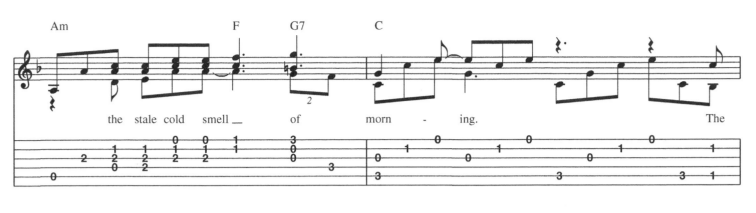

the stale cold smell __ of morn - ing. The

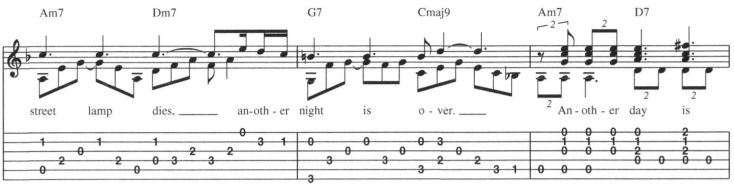

street lamp dies, _____ an-oth-er night is o - ver. _____ An - oth - er day is

Verse

dawn - ing. __ 4. Touch me, _____ it's so eas - y to leave me, _____ all a - lone with the

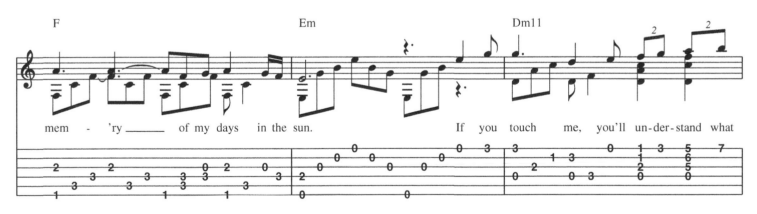

mem - 'ry _____ of my days in the sun. If you touch me, you'll un-der-stand what

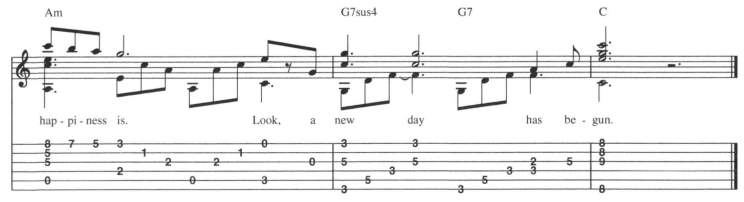

hap - pi - ness is. Look, a new day has be - gun.

My Funny Valentine

from BABES IN ARMS
Words by Lorenz Hart
Music by Richard Rodgers

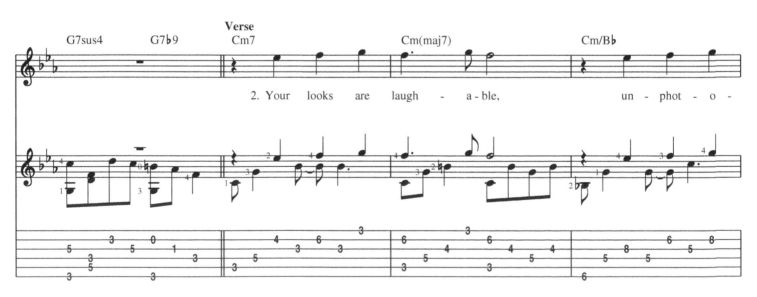

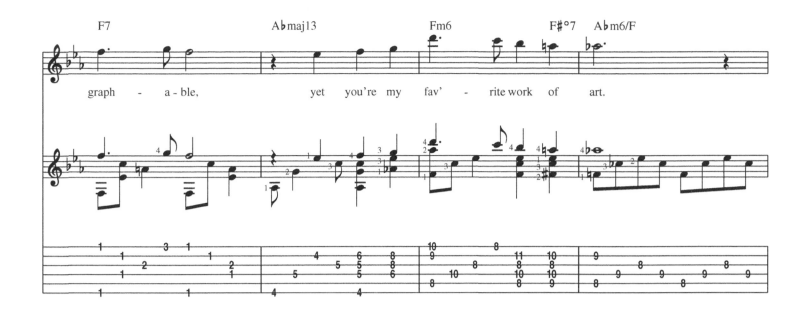

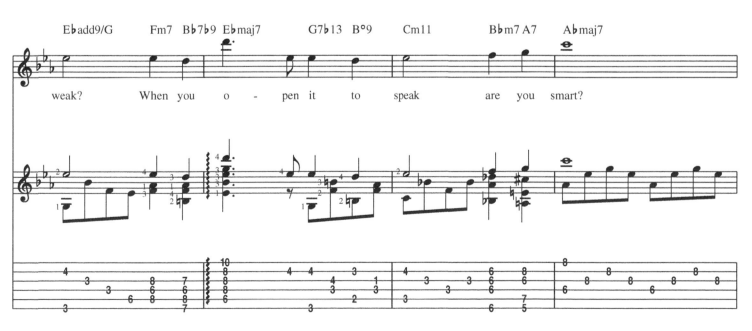

Verse

3. Don't change a hair for me, not if you

care for me. Stay lit - tle Val - en - tine stay.

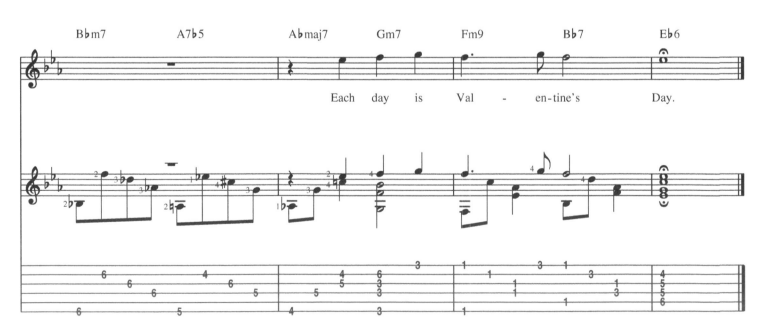

Each day is Val - en - tine's Day.

My Heart Will Go On

(Love Theme From 'Titanic')

from the Paramount and Twentieth Century Fox Motion Picture TITANIC

Music by James Horner

Lyric by Will Jennings

and you're here in my heart, and my heart will go

To Coda ⊕ **Interlude**

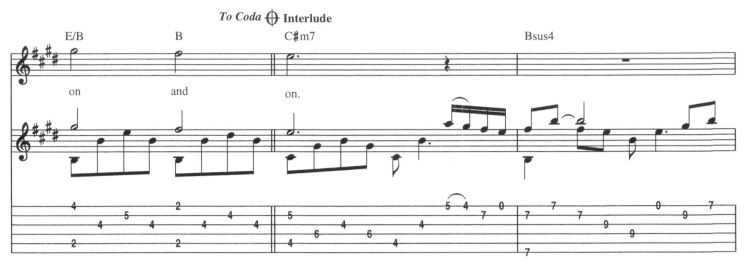

on and on.

Verse

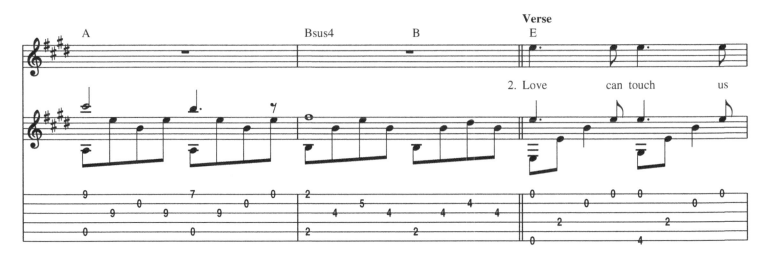

2. Love can touch us

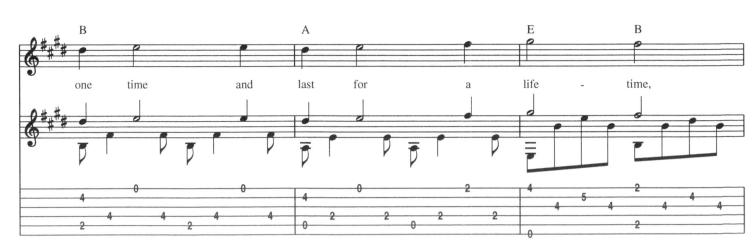

one time and last for a life - time,

D.S. al Coda

Ode to Joy

from SYMPHONY NO. 9 IN D MINOR, FOURTH MOVEMENT CHORAL THEME

Words by Henry van Dyke
Music by Ludwig van Beethoven

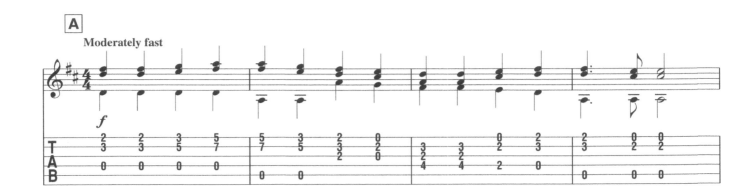

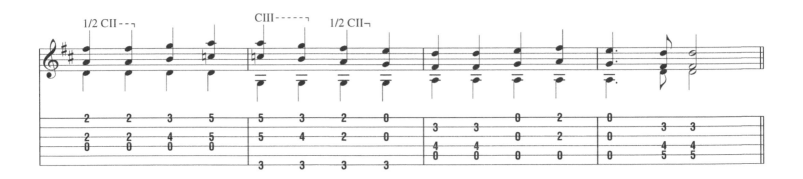

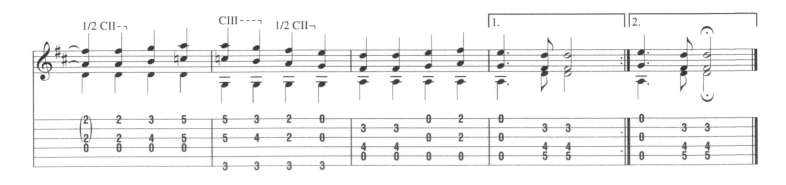

Romance

Anonymous

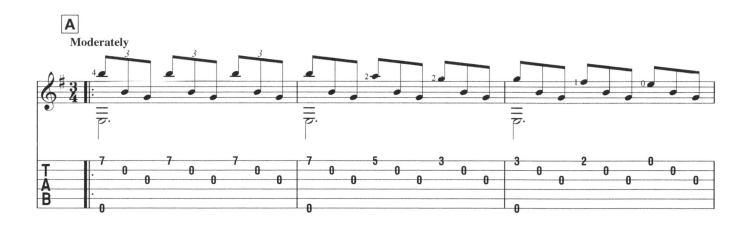

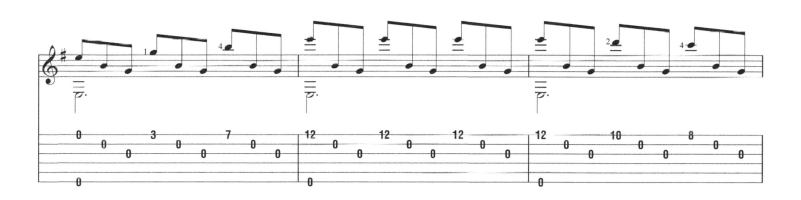

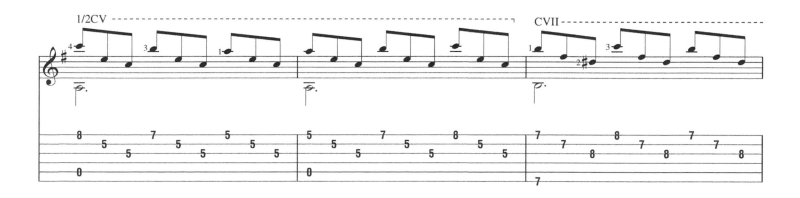

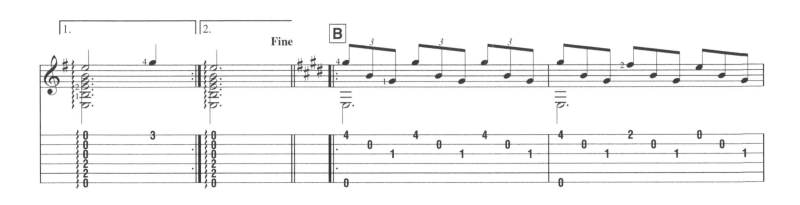

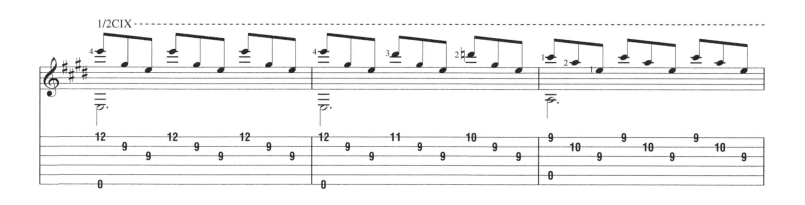

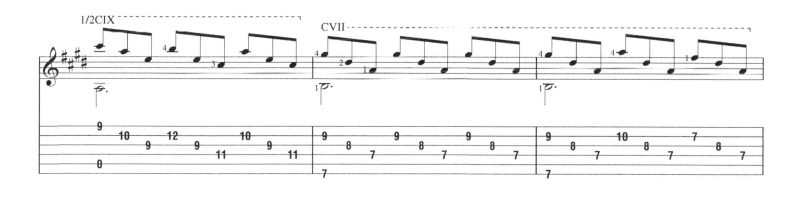

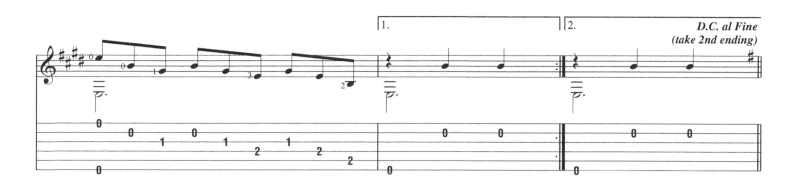

Pomp and Circumstance

Words by Arthur Benson
Music by Edward Elgar

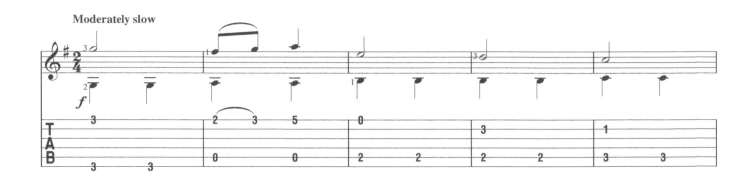

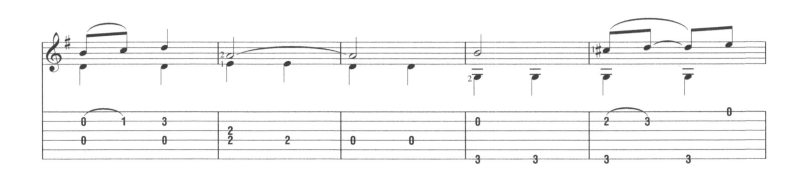

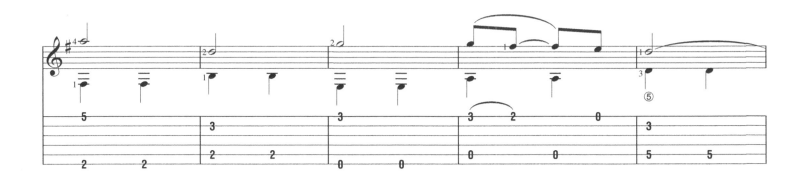

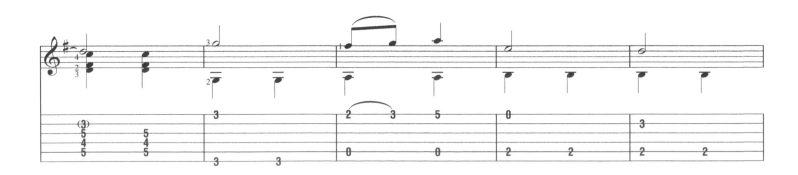

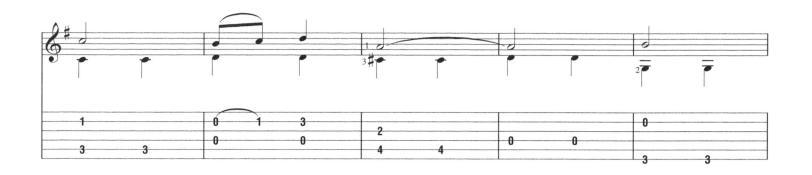

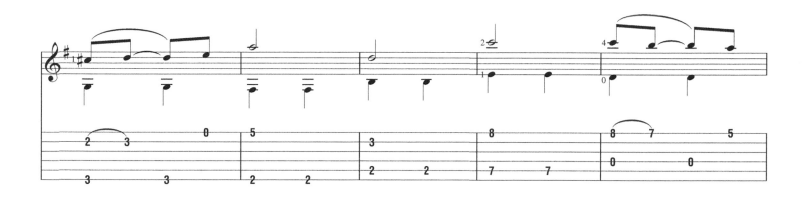

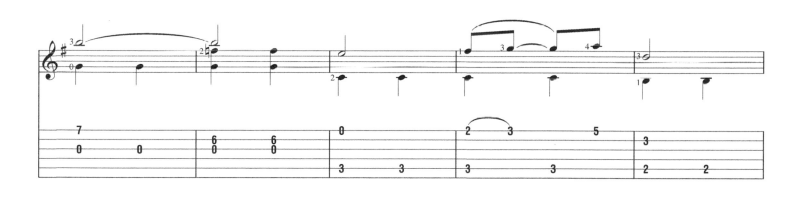

Satin Doll

from SOPHISTICATED LADIES

Words by Johnny Mercer and Billy Strayhorn
Music by Duke Ellington

1. Cig-ar-ette hold-er which wigs me, o-ver her should-er
2. *See additional lyrics*

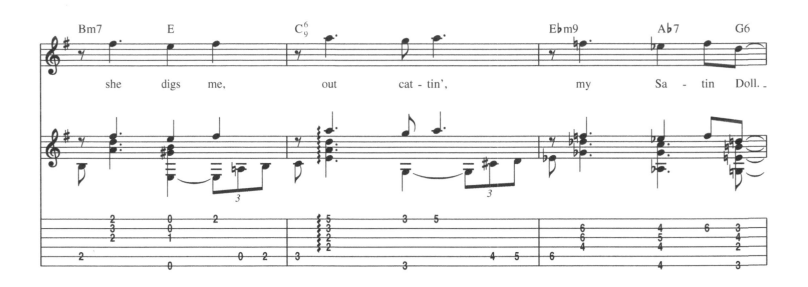

she digs me, out cat-tin', my Sa-tin Doll.

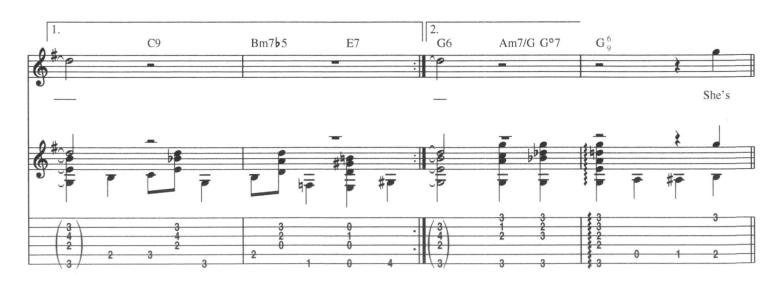

She's

Bridge

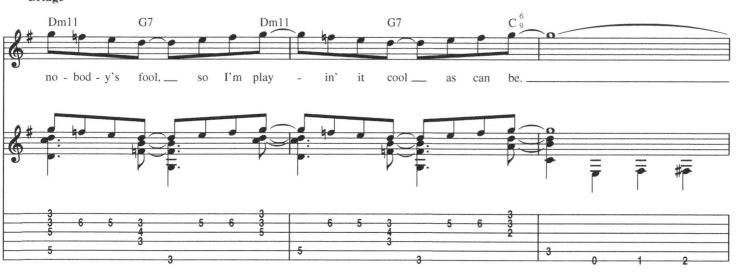

no - bod - y's fool, __ so I'm play - in' it cool __ as can be. __

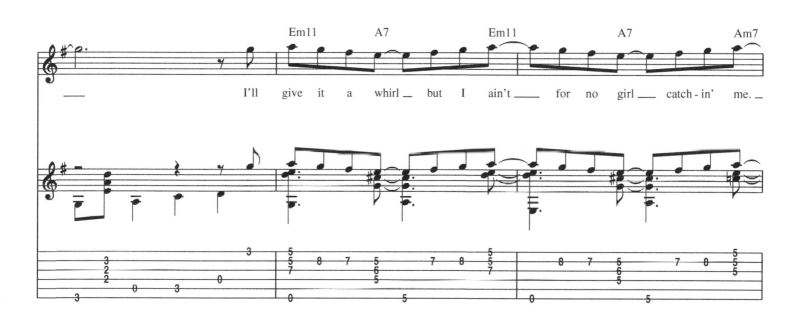

__ I'll give it a whirl __ but I ain't __ for no girl __ catch - in' me. __

Verse

"Switch - e - roo - ney" 3. Tel - e - phone num - bers

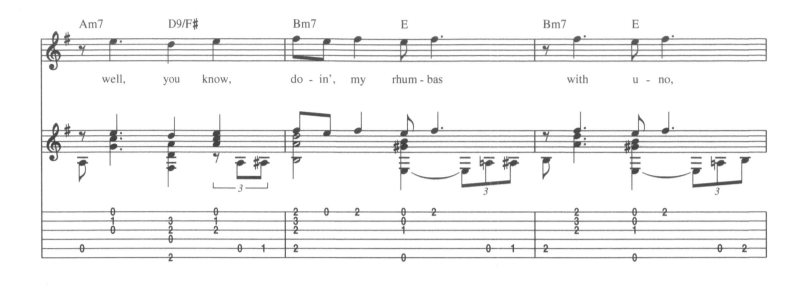

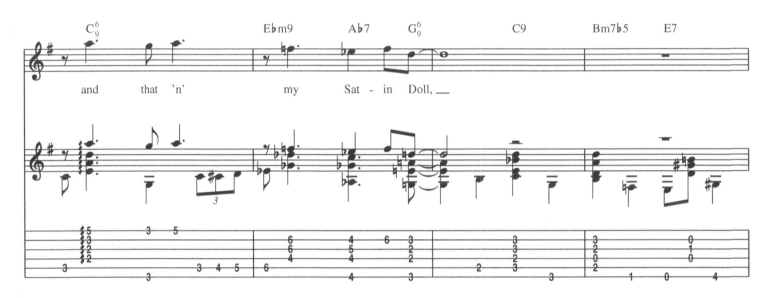

Additional Lyrics

2. Baby, shall we go out skippin'?
Careful, amigo, you're flippin'.
Speaks Latin, my Satin Doll.

Silver Bells

from the Paramount Picture THE LEMON DROP KID

Words and Music by Jay Livingston and Ray Evans

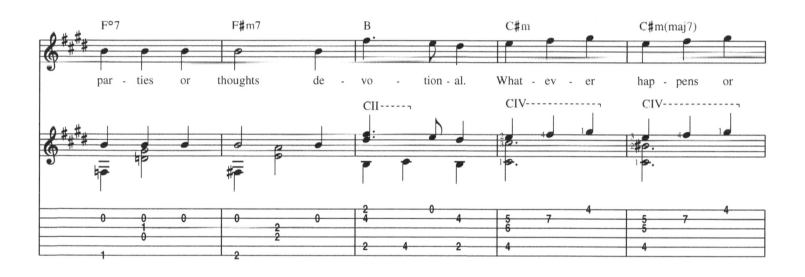

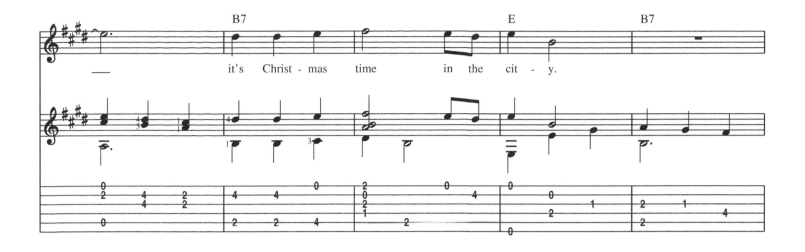

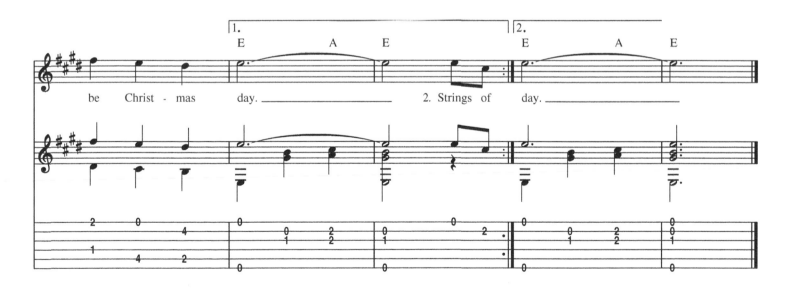

Additional Lyrics

2. Strings of street lights, even stop lights
   Blink a bright red and green,
   As the shoppers rush home with their treasures.
   Hear the snow crunch, see the kids bunch,
   This is Santa's big scene,
   And above all the bustle you hear:

Unchained Melody

Lyric by Hy Zaret
Music by Alex North

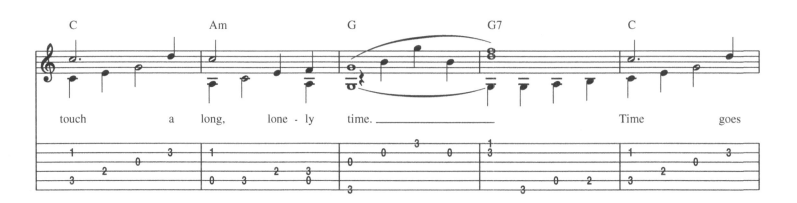

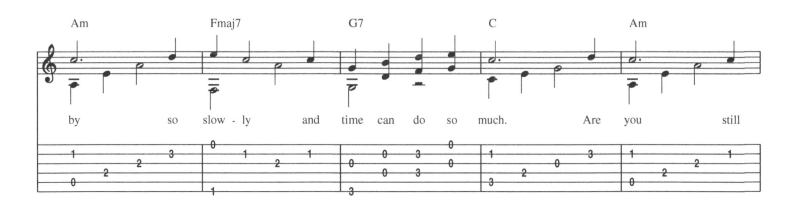

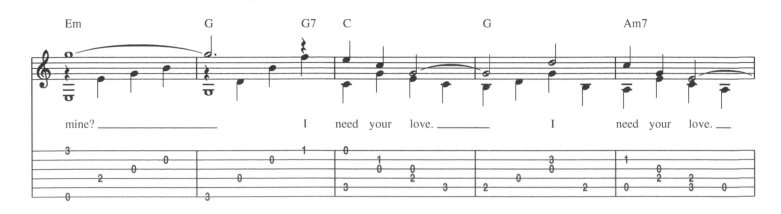

Yesterday

Words and Music by John Lennon and Paul McCartney

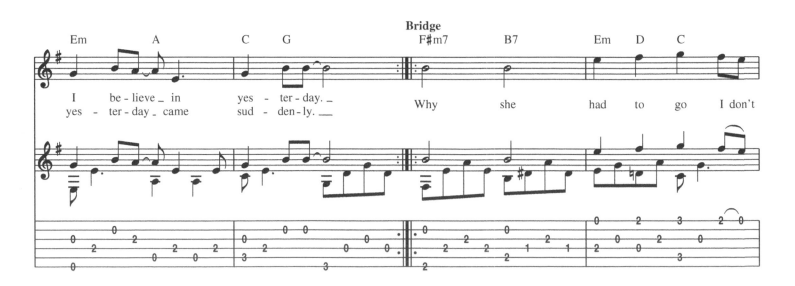

Tears in Heaven

Words and Music by Eric Clapton and Will Jennings

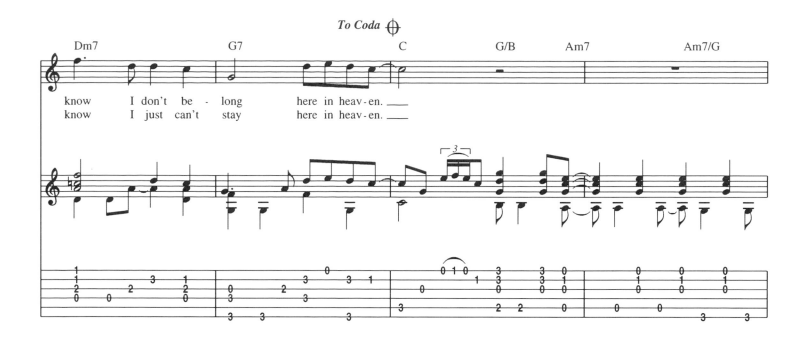

know   I don't be - long   here in heav-en. ____
know   I just can't   stay   here in heav-en. ____

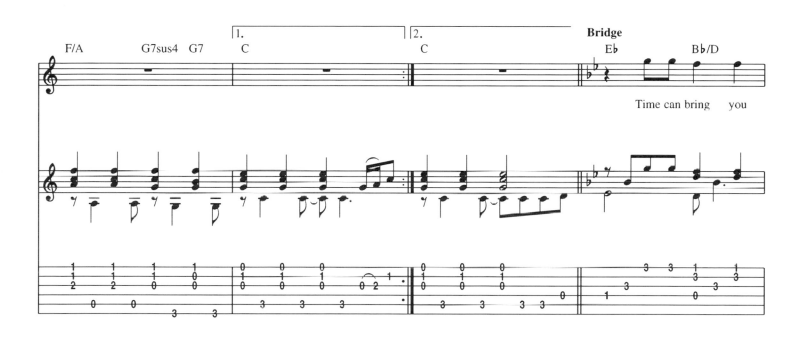

Time can bring   you

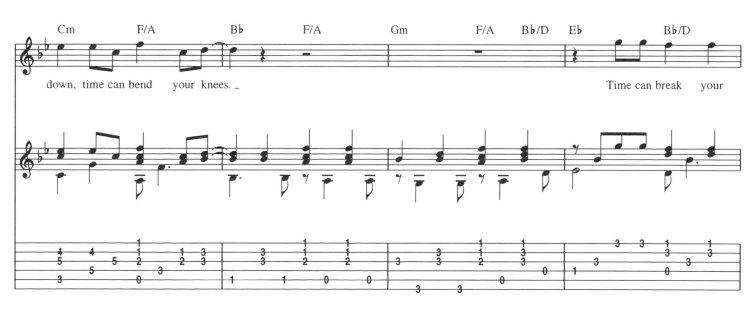

down, time can bend   your knees. _

Time can break   your

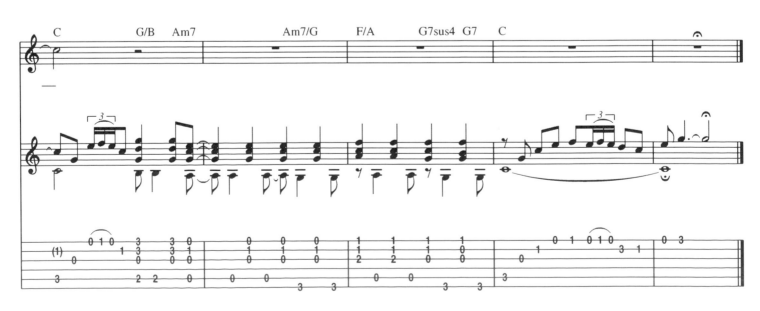